The Playful Way to Serious Writing

Books by Roberta Allen

Fiction

The Traveling Woman

The Daughter

Certain People

The Dreaming Girl

Non Fiction

Amazon Dream

Fast Fiction: Creating Fiction in Five Minutes

The Playful Way to Serious Writing

An Anything-Can-Happen Workbook to Inspire and Delight

Roberta Allen

Houghton Mifflin Company Boston New York 2002

In memory of my father,
and to all my students—past, present, and future

Copyright © 2002 by Roberta Allen
Photographs and drawings by the author

For information about permission to reproduce selections
from this book, write to Permissions, Houghton Mifflin Company,
215 Park Avenue South, New York, New York 10003.

Visit our Web site: www.houghtonmifflinbooks.com.

Library of Congress Cataloging-in-Publication Data is available.

ISBN 0-618-19729-X

Printed in the United States of America

RRD 10 9 8 7 6 5 4

Contents

Starting Out

Looking Inward

Looking Outward

Looking All Around

Looking Ahead

When I was a little girl, drawing saved my life. It allowed me to escape into a world of my own making, a world much happier than the one in which I was raised.

I put so much pressure on the pencil when I drew that I deformed my middle finger. But that still seems to me a small price to pay.

When I look at my finger, I understand the tremendous ENERGY that went into my drawings. That pressure was ENERGY. Sometimes I see my students writing exercises as though their lives depend on it. When I see that, I know they are tapping something important inside themselves.

Often in this book when I use the word ENERGY, I use it to mean the impulse to write. But in the broadest sense, ENERGY to me is life itself.

ENERGY is the force behind the words. It is the power deep inside that drives you. It is the desire to bring forth something that has never before existed. It is the passion to give form to your deepest feelings, your deepest longings, your dreams, your fantasies — who you are.

ENERGY is the spark that ignites when you connect with a place, a creature, a beautiful tree, a sunset, a work of art, a symphony, another human being.

ENERGY is the link between you and something outside yourself that enlarges your world, that changes the way you see, that changes the way you feel.

ENERGY is the invisible force that breaks through when you have an epiphany, when you understand something for the first time — even if it is something painful, something that breaks your heart.

ENERGY is the invisible force that is often locked inside a shell of fear and bursts forth when you break that shell.

ENERGY is the power that is released when you let nothing stop you.

In the late 1970s, after having many exhibitions in the United States and Europe, I didn't feel much ENERGY in making visual art. But I did feel ENERGY when I wrote stories, which came to me in short spurts, often when I was walking down the street. I would stop and write furiously for several minutes in a notebook I carried with me until the ENERGY was spent. Later, I would revise my writing. I wrote an entire book of stories that way.

Since I did not go to college, when I started teaching creative writing after my book was published, I was not programmed to teach writing in any particular way. Instead, I was free to create a method that paralleled my own process of FOLLOWING MY ENERGY.

I did not have the fear I knew many people had about writing. But I had many fears in other areas of my life.

I was nine or ten the day I followed my father's instructions and stood poised at the edge of a pool, ready to dive. The only problem was that I was frozen with fear. "Don't think about it—just do it!" my father said. But unlike the girl in the photo on the right, I couldn't stop my thoughts of fear.

Those words "Don't think about it, just do it!" stayed in my mind. My father had learned them the hard way. When he was a little boy on the Lower East Side, some bigger boys threw him in the East River. He learned how to swim — fast!

My father's experience was extreme to say the least, but I realized years later that pressure forces ENERGY to the surface. This made me think of using a timer with my students. Giving them a time limit would force them to act, not think.

The thinking my father tried to discourage in me is the thinking that stops all of us at one time or another. It is the small critical voice inside that says we don't have what it takes, we don't measure up. It's the voice that keeps us from trying new things. It's the voice that—if we listen—keeps us from living our dreams.

What is the ENERGY METHOD?

The ENERGY METHOD is an instant way to tap in to your creative ENERGY and get your words flowing on paper without interruption.

It is a way to break that shell of fear and write with the exhilaration that comes with releasing pent-up ENERGY.

It is a way to bypass the inner voice that stops you, the critical voice that might make you rework the same sentence all day.

It is a simple, fun-filled way to write that allows you to lose yourself like a child in the magic of creating.

It means going with the words and images that excite you, inspire you.

It means FOLLOWING YOUR CREATIVE ENERGY, following your spark, going wherever it leads you.

When I looked at my first class of students, I saw very serious faces. This must be serious business, I thought, though my class was called "creative" writing. I had always had a lot of fun writing, so I wondered why they couldn't do the same. They looked at me funny, shifting in their seats, when I told them this, but they agreed to do the first of what would be many five-minute exercises. The first was, Write a story about a lie. You have five minutes. Go.

It took only one or two exercises to see their faces lighten up. Some were amazed to find they had written complete stories in that short time span. Others were amazed to be writing at all.

It wasn't the words they wrote that mattered, I told them, but the ENERGY behind the words. Craft can be taught, words can be revised, I said, but ENERGY — the impulse to write — is what really counts. Only by going with your ENERGY can you find what truly inspires you, not only in your writing but in life.

How it works

Set a timer for whatever limit the exercise calls for—anywhere from five to thirty minutes—and write instantly, before you have a chance to think.

The time limit concentrates your ENERGY while the exercise focuses your attention on a particular topic or image.

In the moment you start writing, you are a diver plunging into the unknown.

By letting yourself write freely and spontaneously, you allow your voice to come through and discover, when you let that voice take you in any direction, a sea of unexpected images and associations that might not come to you any other way.

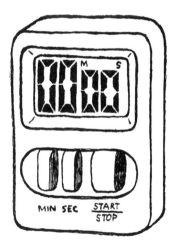

My timer

How to know when a word or image has ENERGY

- You feel the tiniest pinprick of feeling.

- Your eye is drawn to it instantly.

- You find yourself thinking about it.

- It conjures a strong association.

- You feel moved or excited.

- You feel irritated or disturbed.

How to rebel

• Change the time limit. If an exercise calls for ten minutes, do it for five or twenty.

• When asked to pick the third word you've associated with a visual cue, choose the second.

• When asked to write about the word with the most ENERGY, choose another. (You may be surprised to see how much ENERGY there is in a word that is seemingly neutral or, better yet, one you resist.)

How to use the exercises

- as warm-ups

- to generate ideas

- to explore ideas

- to start a project

- to continue a project

- to inject new life in an existing project

- to finish a project

How to choose the exercises

- start anywhere

- start at the beginning

- start in the middle

- start at the end

- jump around

- choose exercises with the most ENERGY

- choose exercises with the least ENERGY

- choose exercises with your eyes closed

In the exercises, you must allow yourself to write whatever comes up—no matter how dark, painful, or downright silly. You must give yourself permission to be as open as a little child. You must give yourself permission to play. If you stop yourself from writing the painful stuff or the silly stuff, you will not get to the real ENERGY—you will not tap in to those things that move you, that make you who you are. You will not have fun with this process, which can help free you from the past.

In this book, not every exercise will have ENERGY for you. Not every one will excite you. When one exercise leaves you cold, do another. Keep doing them until you find the ones I call "triggers," the ones that surprise you, that lead you somewhere you didn't know you wanted to go.

Because an exercise doesn't work for you one time is no reason to believe it won't work for you if you do it again.

Don't automatically bypass exercises that seem to have no ENERGY. Some may have the greatest ENERGY of all.

Splotches

To make this drawing, I loaded my brush with ink, splashed it all over the page, and connected the splotches with lines.

What do you see when you look at this pattern? Write the first six words that come to mind.

1. _____   4. _____

2. _____   5. _____

3. _____   6. _____

Choose the word with the most or least ENERGY or choose number three, set your timer for ten minutes, and go.

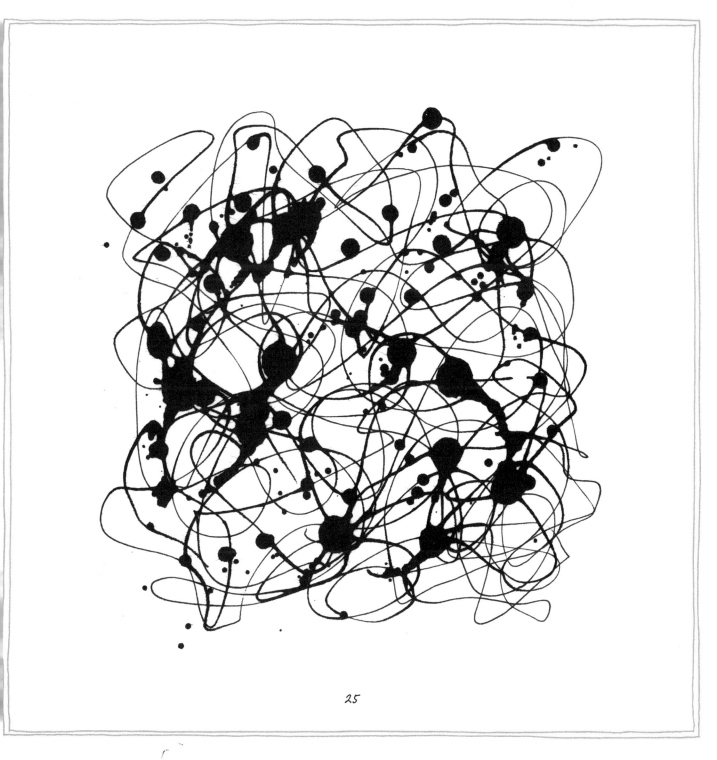

25

What is her secret?

And how is it connected to this house?

Set your timer for fifteen minutes and go!

Pick a letter

Choose the first letter that catches your eye, or point to a letter with closed eyes. Once you've chosen a letter, quickly write six words that begin with that letter.

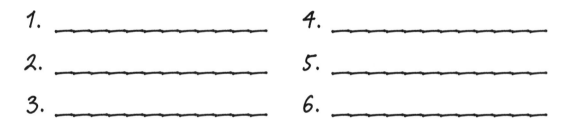

1. _____ 　 4. _____

2. _____ 　 5. _____

3. _____ 　 6. _____

Choose the word with the most or least ENERGY, set your timer for five minutes, and write a piece. Set your timer for ten minutes and write a piece using all six words. Repeat these exercises using the same or a different letter each time.

Why is she smiling?

When I photographed this woman, she had recently left her husband. Is that why she's smiling? Or is there another reason? Set your timer for fifteen minutes and go.

Six figures

On the following pages you will find six figures. Write the first word that comes to mind for each.

1. _____ 4. _____

2. _____ 5. _____

3. _____ 6. _____

Set your timer for five. Write a piece about the word with the most ENERGY. Write one about the word with the least ENERGY in another five-minute piece.

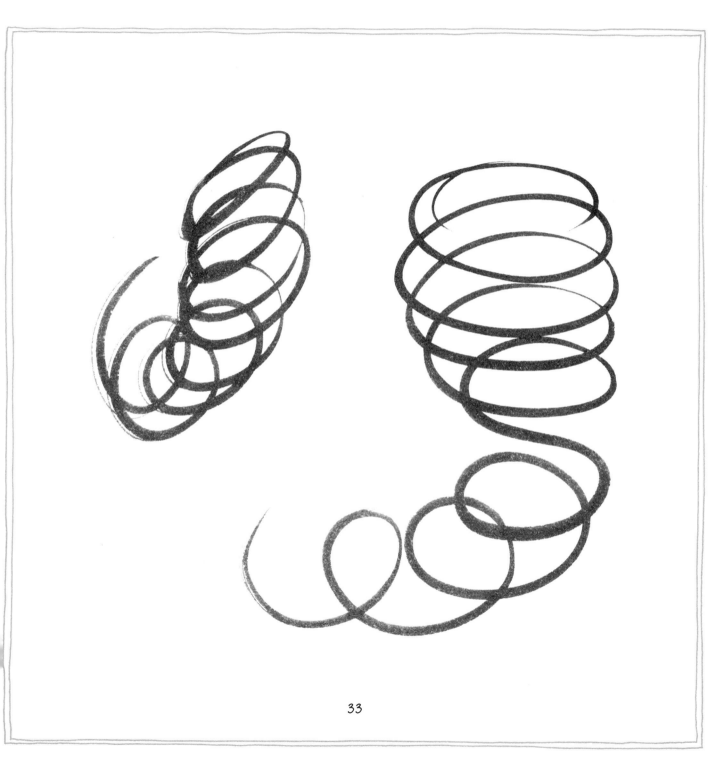

I first thought of writing this book when a former student told me she used my exercises to write her Ph.D. dissertation. An actor I met at a party said she used my exercises to write a screenplay. Students of mine who were also teachers used my exercises in public schools, middle schools, high schools, colleges. Writing conferences used my exercises. So did universities. Workshops and writing groups used them too. People at every level—from fledgling writers to authors of many books—used my exercises to help them write.

My first book on writing, <u>Fast Fiction</u>, was limited to fiction writing, but, on their own, some people were discovering they could use my method to write more than short short stories, short stories, or even novels. Why not make this method available, I thought, to people who want to write memoirs, creative nonfiction, personal essays, plays, screenplays, monologues, performance pieces, prose poems, sketches, journals—you name it!

I thought too about my own experiences and how I might use them as well to help people write.

Moments

One day in New York, I was in a bad mood while crossing a small park. It was raining. Suddenly I looked up. In wonder I saw, silhouetted against a gray sky, a tree with long, slender black pods that looked like calligraphic writing.

Think of small moments in your life that had ENERGY — that made you feel alive. Make a list on the right-hand page. Set your timer for five minutes, choose one, and go.

In the next week, notice small moments that move you. Make a list. When you're ready, set your timer for five minutes, and write about one.

Old Moments

1. _____

2. _____

3. _____

4. _____

5. _____

New Moments

1. _____

2. _____

3. _____

4. _____

5. _____

List moments as succinctly as possible.

How far back can you go? Imagine yourself descending these stairs into your past. What do you recall? Set your timer for five minutes and write a piece about the earliest memory that comes to mind.

Memories

Think of five events from the past, positive or negative, that moved you intensely. These events had great ENERGY at the time.

1. _____

2. _____

3. _____

4. _____

5. _____

Pick the one with the most ENERGY, the one that is most alive for you now. Set your timer for fifteen minutes and write about it.

I had no desire to go to college. It wasn't that I didn't want to learn. I did. Most of all I wanted to learn how to paint. But I wanted to do it MY way. So I got a job, moved to the Village, saved a little money, then went to Europe by myself.

I traveled to many countries, absorbing the light, the air, the colors, before I decided to paint in Amsterdam, where, less than a year later, I had my first solo show.

More memories

Think of five times in your life when you accomplished exactly what you set out to do.

1. _____

2. _____

3. _____

4. _____

5. _____

Set your timer for five minutes and write a piece about the one with the most ENERGY.

When I was eight, my father sent me to summer camp. He wanted me to be like other children. But before that could happen, I had to learn to do things by myself. My bunkmates laughed at me until I learned how to tie my shoes, wash myself, make my bed, fold my clothes. My mother and grandmother had kept me helpless and dependent. My first summer at camp was painful, but it changed my life.

Whose memory is it?

List three painful memories.

1. _____

2. _____

3. _____

Imagine a character below recalling one of your memories as though it is his or her own. Set your timer for five and go.

a shoplifter	a college sophomore	a horse trainer
a holistic healer	an eighth-grader	a wealthy widow
a retired engineer	a clown	a blind man

Continue choosing characters and writing five-minute exercises until the memory seems less painful.

False memories

Imagine five characters accomplishing exactly what each one set out to do.

1. _____

2. _____

3. _____

4. _____

5. _____

Set your timer for five minutes and write a piece about the one with the most ENERGY.

Still more memories

Think of five times in your life when you let fear stop you.

1. _____

2. _____

3. _____

4. _____

5. _____

Set your timer for five minutes and write about the one with the most ENERGY.

Two sides of the story

What does this boy remember about the woman on the right-hand page? Was she important in his life? Set your timer for ten and go.

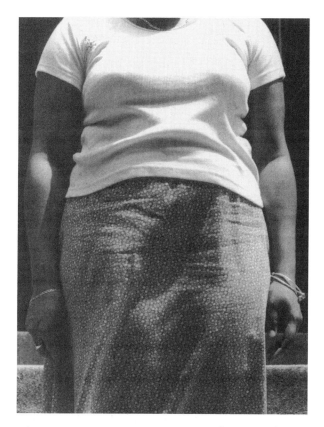

What does this woman remember about this boy? Was he important in her life? Set your timer for ten and go.

The fact that the ENERGY METHOD can be used for so many different kinds of writing inspired me to expand it. This time I decided to pull all the plugs and see how far I could go in designing a book that would let you be as free and creative as you've always wanted to be by tapping in to that ENERGY inside you and bringing forth those feelings, longings, dreams that connect all of us, not only to one another but to life.

Expect to produce writing that has ENERGY, that comes from the core of who you are.

Expect to produce more writing than you ever thought possible, whether you start from scratch on long or short projects, continue old projects, or use the exercises just to play. You need not have any goal other than your pure enjoyment.

Expect to have fun and feel free. Anything can happen! Expect to surprise yourself over and over again.

I learned the power of the ENERGY METHOD from one of my first private students: a young man who came to me with a completed novel that had taken him two years to write. The problem was that the words had no ENERGY. They were just words. They lacked life.

He agreed to start over and do my timed exercises. In six weeks a novel began to emerge that was so strong and beautifully written I knew he had tapped something deep within himself.

What I learned is that anyone who spends two years writing has something to say. But the real writing comes only when the ENERGY is unlocked.

When he did the exercises, he got in touch with the real source of his impulse to write. The source was a traumatic experience. When he was thirteen, he saved his little sister and himself from their psychotic mother.

Although his situation is extreme, he confirmed my belief that the need to write—the ENERGY—arises in many instances out of an unconscious need to complete something from the past. I believe our need to write is part of our larger need to understand who we are and what we feel.

A safe place

Imagine this as a safe place.

This place may be larger than Texas, as big as Australia, or the size of your living room.

Set your timer for thirty minutes. Write (on as many sheets as you need) anything you're afraid to write about, feel guilty writing about, feel foolish writing about, or have any reservations writing about whatsoever.

Objects not directly related

Connect the tricycle and the torn sandal in a piece.

Set your timer for five or ten minutes and go!

When I was a child, I was left alone with my anxious grandmother while my mother worked. I was not allowed to play with other children, except on Sundays, when my father — a gambler — was not running from the Mafia or the Internal Revenue Service.

Under the watchful eyes of my grandmother, I drew hundreds of faces. Those faces were my companions, my friends. I made up stories about them.

My mother and grandmother were afraid of everything. They taught me to be afraid too. "Don't touch the floor! It's dirty," they said. They talked about germs and sickness and how I might fall and hurt myself roller-skating with my father.

Pick a fear

Use your fears to get creative. Write down eight fears that come to mind.

1. _____

2. _____

3. _____

4. _____

5. _____

6. _____

7. _____

8. _____

Set your timer for ten minutes and write about the fear with the most ENERGY.

Set your timer for five minutes and write about the same fear from a different point of view. Choose one from the list on the following page. Imagine that person sharing your fear or taking an objective view of it. Repeat this exercise using four different points of view.

You may do these exercises for each fear on your list.

a parolee

a park ranger

an ex-teen idol

a CEO

a firefighter's widow

a club bouncer

a cheating husband

a marine

a baby

a Greek goddess

a talk show host

a tour leader

a spelling champion

a gospel singer

a society hostess

a senile grandmother

a serial killer

a guru

a stalker

an old hippie

a camp counselor

a rookie cop

a dog walker

More fears

When I finally let go and dove into a pool twenty years after my initial attempt, I felt instantly free. How did I do it? I dove in very fast — before that little voice inside had a chance to stop me.

Think of four fears you have overcome.

1. _____

2. _____

3. _____

4. _____

Set your timer for five minutes and write about the one with the most ENERGY.

Still more fears

Sometimes it is easier to write about other people's fears. Here are some from my students' lists:

- fear of cooking chicken
- fear of deep water
- fear of meeting new people
- fear of being yelled at
- fear of making phone calls
- fear of swift movement
- fear of balloons

Set your timer and write about the fear with the most ENERGY for five minutes.

Before you do more exercises, know that there is no wrong way to do them as long as you FOLLOW YOUR ENERGY.

You will find on the following pages hundreds of exercises that can be used over and over with vastly different results.

If your writing "takes off" and there is enough ENERGY to sustain it without a timer, feel free to even abandon the timer—until you need it again.

What will happen here?

Set your timer for ten minutes and go!

Found objects

Who found these mannequin hands? Where? Why did he or she want them? Set your timer for five and go.

My artistic talent was a given. I was born with it. My mother told me I drew perfect circles when I was three. Whether this is true or not, I don't know. I only know that my father was very proud of my drawing.

I don't know where I got the idea that it wasn't okay to write. But it was only when I was an adult exhibiting my art in Europe that I realized I had stopped myself from writing for years because I didn't want to be better than my father. He came to New York as a poor Russian immigrant and never went beyond third grade. Though he ran a business and had no trouble reading racing forms, he never learned how to write much more than his name.

Realizations

After realizing that I had stopped myself from writing because I didn't want to be better than my father, I started writing stories, which changed my life.

Think of five realizations that changed your life or could have changed your life. Maybe you realized you didn't love your boyfriend but married him anyway. Realizations have ENERGY!

If you can't think of "big" realizations, think of "little" ones. Maybe you realized your little brother wasn't so bad when he lied for you to your parents.

If you can't think of any realizations, make them up!

Remember—when you have a realization, you are aware of something you weren't aware of before.

After you list your realizations below, pick the one with the most ENERGY, set your timer for ten minutes, and write about it.

1. _____

2. _____

3. _____

4. _____

5. _____

Life-shaping events

Think of the events that shaped your life. There are only a few of them. One might be your marriage, another the birth of a child. Another might be the loss of a parent, or a serious illness. List five.

1. _____

2. _____

3. _____

4. _____

5. _____

Set your timer for five minutes and write about the one with the most ENERGY.

Imagine a character below weighing one of the events that shaped your life. Is the character sympathetic? Neutral? Antagonistic?

an FBI agent
a sixth-grader
a traveler
a bridesmaid
a Mets fan

a pregnant teen
a scuba diver
a dog or cat
a window cleaner
a car thief

Set your timer for ten minutes and go. Continue choosing characters and writing ten-minute exercises until you see the event with new eyes.

Found objects

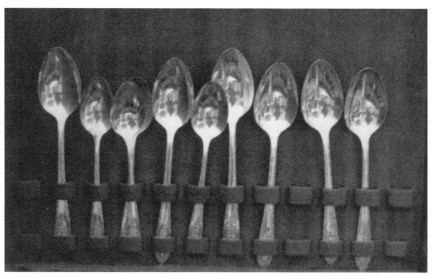

Where are the missing spoons? Set your timer for five and go.

Woman sitting

What has she realized about herself while sitting here? Set your timer for ten and go.

Decisions

Quickly list four decisions you made recently or in the past. Maybe you decided to buy a car or leave your girlfriend or sell a house or go back to school. Or maybe you just decided to switch dry cleaners or eat fish on Fridays.

1. _____

2. _____

3. _____

4. _____

Choose the decision with the most ENERGY. Set your timer for ten minutes and write a piece about your decision.

More decisions

Look at the four decisions on the previous page. Now imagine yourself making the opposite decision in each instance. Write the opposite decisions below.

1. _____

2. _____

3. _____

4. _____

Choose the opposite decision with the most ENERGY, set your timer for ten, and write a piece imagining the possible consequences.

Still more decisions

What surprising decisions has this woman made?
What good decisions? What bad decisions?

Did she decide to leave her husband for a
younger man? Did she become a vegetarian? Did
she decide not to ask for something she wants?

Set your timer for fifteen minutes and write
about one or more decisions she made.

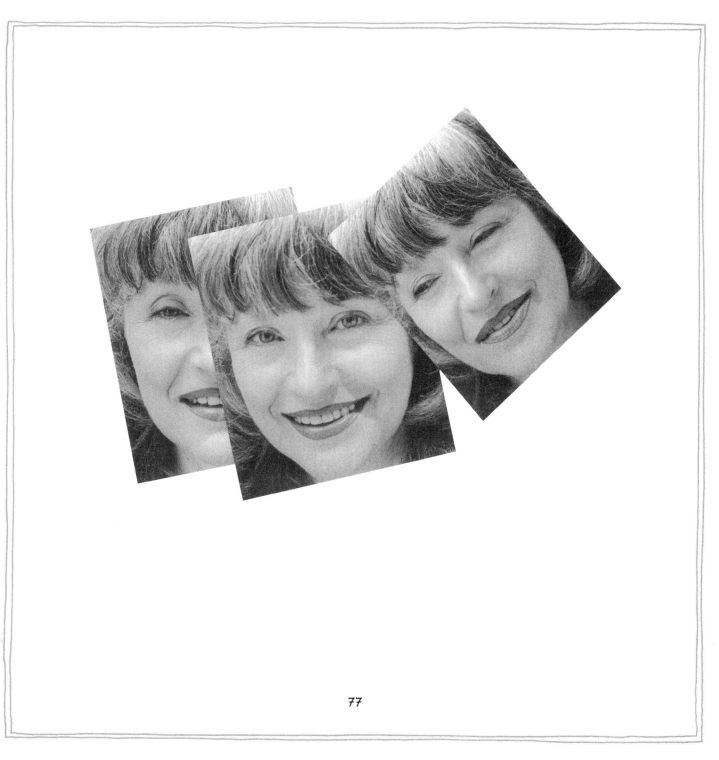

What does he want?

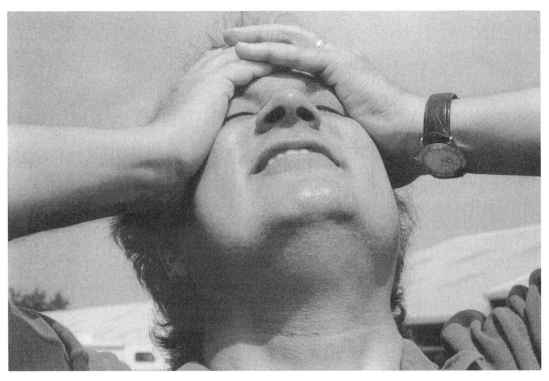

When he closes his eyes, does he see himself as
a famous artist? A ladies' man? The owner of a
transatlantic shipping line? Set your timer for
ten and write about this man.

Desires

Quickly list five things you want, someone you know wants, or a character wants.

1. _____

2. _____

3. _____

4. _____

5. _____

Choose the one with the most or least ENERGY, set your timer for ten, and write about it. Include the consequences of getting it or not getting it.

When I was a little girl, I dreamt of going to the Amazon. I imagined the Amazon as a wild place far away from my mother and grandmother, where I could get dirty and do as I pleased. The jungle was so deep they would never find me.

Many years later, I decided to live my childhood dream and go to the Amazon alone. I didn't listen to the little voice that said I couldn't do it. I went in spite of my fear. I carried a duffel full of pharmaceuticals to protect me from creatures and diseases with names I couldn't pronounce. I hired guides and made river trips and lived one of the great adventures of my life.

Dreams

What do you dream of doing? Climbing Mount Everest? Flying a plane? Finding the perfect relationship? List five of your dreams.

1. _____
2. _____
3. _____
4. _____
5. _____

Set your timer for five minutes and write about the one with the most ENERGY.

Imaginary dreams

Imagine five characters. What is each one's dream? Does a single mom dream of going to college? Does a handicapped man dream of finding his long-lost sister? List the characters and their dreams.

1. _____

2. _____

3. _____

4. _____

5. _____

Set your timer for five minutes and write about the one with the most ENERGY.

Pick a letter

When I first started writing, I made up games for myself. I loved (and still love) the way words sound, so I would take random letters of the alphabet like "C," for instance, and write a quick story using as many words as I could think of starting with the letter "C."

Choose the letter with the most or least ENERGY or pick one with your eyes closed. Set your timer for five minutes and write a piece using as many words as you can that begin with your chosen letter.

Who and where?

Write a piece connecting this woman with the door on the right. Is she behind this door? What is happening? Does she see this door in a dream? Set your timer for ten and go.

Loose lines

It took many years for me to break free and draw lines as loose as these. When I was a child, my drawings were very tight, very neat, very controlled. I wasn't allowed to be messy. I wasn't allowed to get my hands dirty.

Set your timer for fifteen minutes. Let yourself be as loose as these lines. Write whatever comes to mind as you look at them.

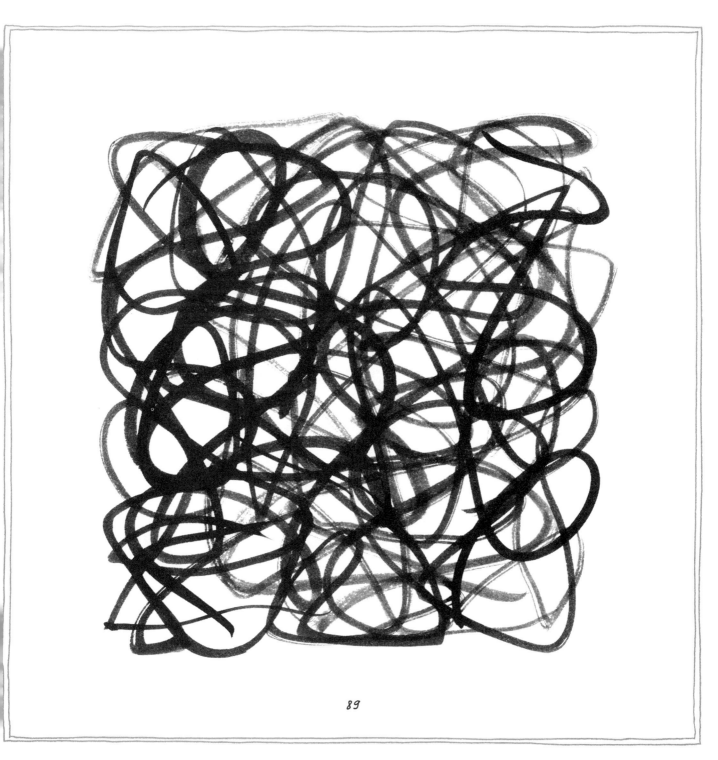

Three ways to explore characters or real people on the following pages

1. Combine a real person or character in your writing with characters he or she is unlikely to meet by doing exercises in PICK A CHARACTER, starting on page 94.

2. Imagine one or more real people or characters in your writing in unlikely settings by using them in exercises from PICK A PLACE, starting on page 148.

3. Imagine a real person or character in your writing having one of the MINOR MISHAPS on page 105.

Ten ways to get a piece or project unstuck

1. Find a word or phrase in the last part you've written with the merest hint of ENERGY and use it as a "trigger" to continue where you left off. Set your timer for five and go.

2. Choose a random word or phrase in the last part you've written and use it as a "trigger" to continue where you left off. Set your timer for five.

3. Find the last sentence that had ENERGY. Discard everything after that. Set your timer for ten and use that sentence as a "trigger" to continue.

4. Choose an exercise unrelated to your piece or project. Set your timer for five and connect that exercise. DO NOT THINK ABOUT <u>HOW</u> TO CONNECT IT BEFORE YOU WRITE. Just choose it, set your timer for five, and go.

5. Choose an exercise that could be related to your piece or project. Set your timer for five and connect it.

6. Imagine someone <u>other</u> than your protagonist. Substitute that person or character for the one in your piece or project. Set your timer for ten or fifteen and see what happens.

7. Rearrange your piece or project. Put the middle at the end, the end at the beginning, the beginning in the middle. For long works, set your timer for thirty minutes, for shorter ones fifteen, for short pieces five.

8. Continue your piece or project by adding a person or character. Set your timer for ten and go.

9. Eliminate a person or character. Set your timer for five or ten minutes and go.

10. Change the setting or add a setting. Set your timer for ten or fifteen minutes and go.

Pick a character

On the following pages, choose one with the most or least ENERGY or choose one that feels neutral. Or pick one with closed eyes. Set your timer for five and go.

On the following pages, choose four any way you want to. Combine the four characters in a twenty-minute exercise.

a bird watcher

a rebellious student

a repairman with a grudge

a defense lawyer

a bad boy

a landlord with sinus trouble

an accident victim

a woman with ten dogs

a personal trainer

a self-destructive brother

a Mets catcher

an anorexic mother

an abusive bully

a bus passenger

a sour-faced son

a middle-aged loner

a voyeur

a lap dancer

an amnesiac

an actor with a glass eye

a cheating tenth-grader

a stamp collector

a minister's wife

a bike messenger

a chain-smoker

a suspicious hotel manager

a deaf hairdresser

a sneaky choirboy

a hiker

an embryo

a paranoid redneck

a gambler

a woman who saves newspapers

a professional gigolo in Paris

a priest

a debutante

a betrayed lover

a traveler

a deliveryman

an inventor

a political activist

a Holocaust survivor

an earthquake survivor

a shy beekeeper

a drunk

a Danish filmmaker

a voice teacher

a missing person

a reluctant volunteer

an art collector

a football fan

an acrobat

a dizzy waiter

a binger

a Boy Scout

a champagne-drinking wannabe

a homeless person

a Rollerblading insomniac

a reckless driver

the widow of a phony war hero

a moucher

a butcher

an illiterate miner

a millionaire

a religious fanatic

a British upper-class bore

a pleasure-loving bigamist

an Oscar nominee

a sculptor with a limp

Who have I left out?

Invent your own characters. List them quickly on the left-hand side. On the right, rate them in terms of ENERGY: 1 has the most ENERGY, 6 has the least.

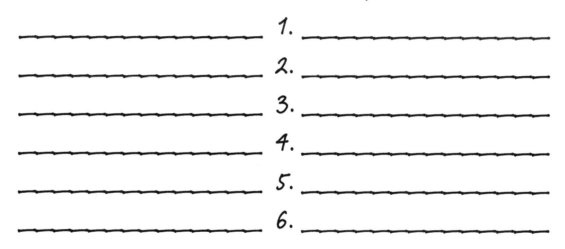

1. _____
2. _____
3. _____
4. _____
5. _____
6. _____

Set your timer for five. Write about the one with the most ENERGY. Then set your timer for twenty and write a piece about two or three of your other characters.

who and where?

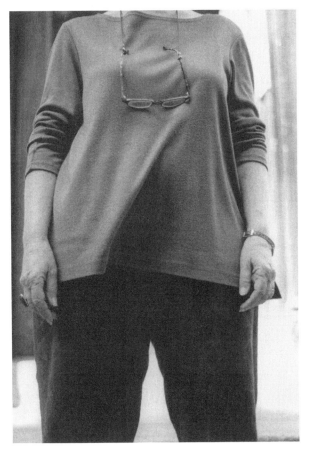

Write a piece connecting this woman and this place.

Set your timer for ten minutes and go.

Getting physical

Set your timer for ten minutes. Write about someone real or imagined who has one or more of the physical characteristics listed on the following page. How has one or more of these characteristics affected this person's life?

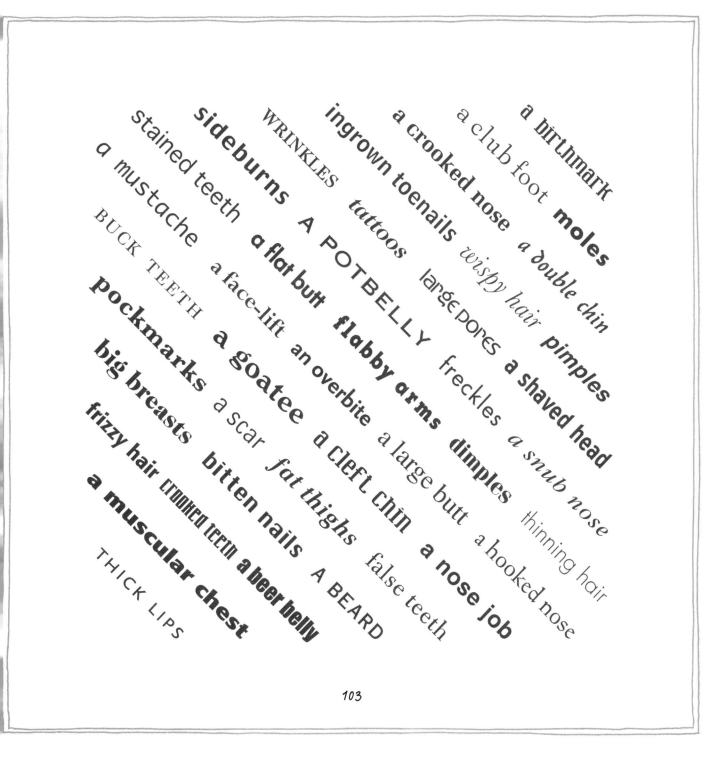

a birthmark

a club foot **moles**

a crooked nose a double chin

ingrown toenails

WRINKLES tattoos large pores a shaved head

sideburns A POTBELLY

stained teeth

a mustache **a flat butt flabby arms** freckles a snub nose

a face-lift an overbite **dimples** thinning hair

BUCK TEETH

pockmarks a goatee a large butt a hooked nose

wispy hair **pimples**

a crooked nose

big breasts a scar fat thighs a cleft chin **a nose job**

frizzy hair CROOKED TEETH **a beer belly** A BEARD false teeth

bitten nails

a muscular chest

THICK LIPS

103

getting drenched in a storm   *bumping into*
someone   burning the roast   dialing the wrong number
dropping a cut-glass bowl   spilling coffee   **being late**
tearing a sweater on a nail   **failing math**   *ringing the wrong*
bell   getting lost   **following the wrong person**   tripping
over a toy   **throwing the ball out of bounds**
taking the wrong road   **telling a bad joke**   getting off
at the wrong stop   buying the wrong size   cutting a finger
catching a zipper   missing a cue   *losing money*
stepping in a puddle   *saying the wrong thing*
singing off key   driving off the road   chipping a tooth

Minor mishaps

Or are they? You may write about an incident from your own life, someone else's life, or make up an incident.

What are the consequences of the act you've chosen? Set your timer for fifteen minutes and go.

If you choose, you may write about two or three mishaps in a single piece. Set your timer for twenty minutes and go.

Shades of gray

I like to think life is simple; that everything is either black or white. But it rarely turns out that way.

Write the first six words that come to mind when you look at this drawing.

1. _____   4. _____

2. _____   5. _____

3. _____   6. _____

Set your timer for fifteen and choose the word with the most ENERGY as the subject of your piece.

Recently, in the park at the top of a hill, I saw a terrified little girl trying to learn how to ride a bicycle. Her father, holding it steady, said over and over, "I won't let go. I promise." The girl screamed, "YES YOU WILL! YOU WILL—JUST LIKE BEFORE!" I knew exactly how she felt. I realized then that I had never trusted my father. Our Sundays in the park were often ordeals. But without him to challenge me, I would never have broken free from my mother and grandmother.

My father wanted me to excel at sports and called me "Butchy." He wanted me to be brave and strong. He loved me, but I don't think he knew how to relate to a girl child. It took many years for me to realize that what I wanted more  than going to the Amazon was to be the little girl with a pink plastic pocketbook and a lilac patterned dress (but that would have meant being like my mother and grandmother). Long after my father's death (to keep him with me perhaps), I challenged myself—as he had challenged me— by traveling all over the world to places that scared me but also made me feel alive.

Pick a problem

Choose one of the lines on the following pages and incorporate it in a five-minute piece. The line may appear at the beginning, the middle, or the end.

I shouldn't be here.

Is he following me?

This is the wrong size.

It's not supposed to look like this.

What has she done?

Where did he go?

Should I act as though everything is okay?

It's stuck.

It's not supposed to be like this.

I lost it.

It shouldn't be.

Should I go with him?

I can't do it.

There's no one here by that name.

My sister doesn't understand.

It won't come out.

Do you know me?

My daughter isn't home yet.

No one knows where he is.

You can't leave now.

Suppose he finds out.

I can't tell her.

How could she say that?

Where did he go?

How can I prove she's wrong about me?

I won't let him do it.

What did I do to deserve this?

No one will believe it.

What should I do?

Why did this happen to him?

How did this happen?

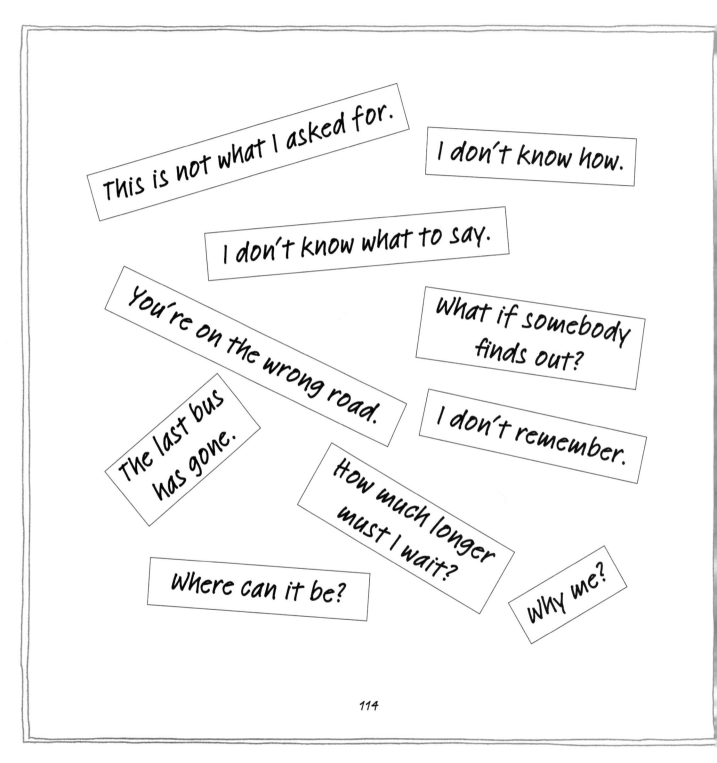

This is not what I asked for.

I don't know how.

I don't know what to say.

What if somebody finds out?

You're on the wrong road.

I don't remember.

The last bus has gone.

How much longer must I wait?

Where can it be?

Why me?

More problems

In the left-hand column, make up your own list of problems — quickly! Set your timer for two minutes and go! They may be real or imaginary problems. Now, in the right-hand column, rate them in terms of ENERGY, 1 is the highest, 6 is the lowest.

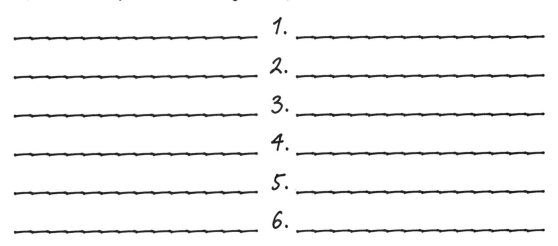

_____ 1. _____

_____ 2. _____

_____ 3. _____

_____ 4. _____

_____ 5. _____

_____ 6. _____

Now choose one. Set your timer for five or ten minutes and go!

Take a problem from the previous page and imagine how one of the following would deal with it:

an astrologer	a child
a high school principal	a homeless person
a therapist	a police officer
a mother	a ballerina
a zoologist	a firefighter
a psychic advisor	an uncle

Set your timer for five minutes and go. When you finish, choose another. Write for another five minutes. Do this until the problem seems either funny, solvable, or inconsequential.

What is his problem?

And why is he wearing long pants? Is he rebellious? Abused? Hyperactive? Overprotected? Set your timer for ten and write about this boy.

Are "they" the same man? If so, what has happened to him between the time this picture was taken on the beach and the time this

picture was taken in the city? If they are two men, who are they and how are they connected? Set your timer for fifteen and go.

Solutions

Below are the solutions to twelve problems. Choose the one with the most or least ENERGY and write the problem after setting your timer for fifteen minutes.

1. leaving town for good
2. ending a friendship
3. telling the truth about his wife
4. paying $20,000
5. tearing up his telephone number
6. getting engaged
7. looking for a new job
8. letting go of anger
9. buying a house
10. joining the Marines
11. playing the saxophone
12. borrowing money

Mixed feelings

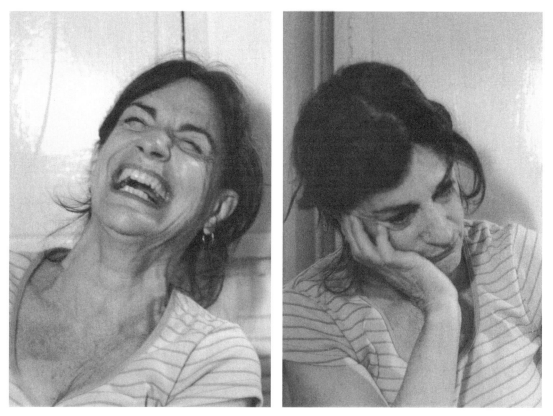

What makes her laugh? What makes her sad? Set your timer for fifteen minutes and write about this woman.

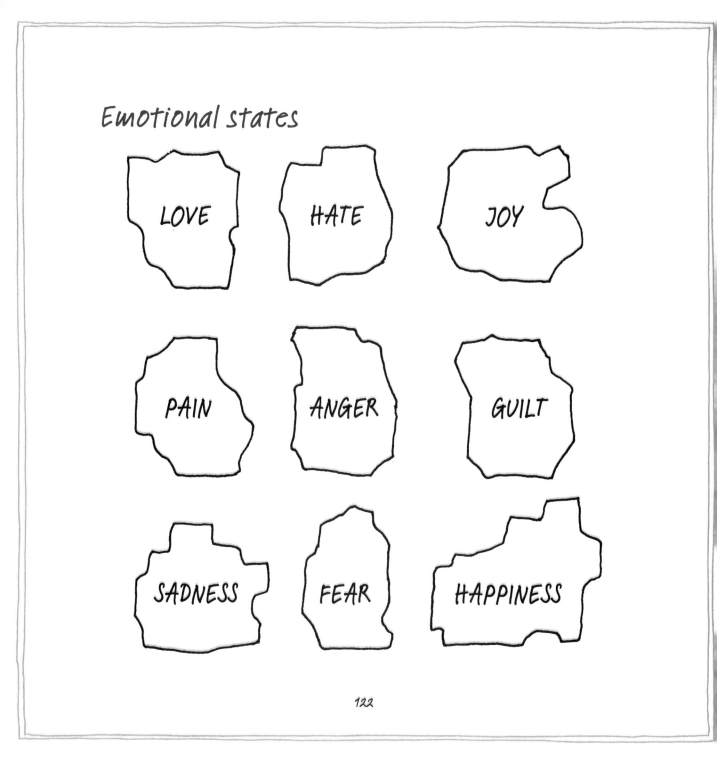

Emotional states

LOVE   HATE   JOY

PAIN   ANGER   GUILT

SADNESS   FEAR   HAPPINESS

More emotional states

Jealousy	Fulfillment	Exhaustion
Rage	Irritation	Remorse
Compulsiveness	Despair	Amazement
Humiliation	Tension	Childishness
Tenderness	Peacefulness	Confusion
Shock	Serenity	Rapture
Wonder	Passion	Morbidity
Ambivalence	Playfulness	Grief
Annoyance	Satisfaction	Pleasure
Shame	Embarrassment	Agitation

On a separate sheet, you may add to this list any other emotional states that come to mind. Then choose one with the most or least ENERGY from the left-hand page, this page, or your own list; set your timer for twenty minutes; and write a piece.

A stranger

When I photographed this man, I didn't know if he was asleep, daydreaming, or merely listening to the live band playing in the park that day. Who is he? What is going on in his life? Set your timer for twenty and go.

Mirror monologue

What is going through her mind as she looks in the mirror? Is she dreaming about someone? Remembering? Making plans? Set your timer for five and go.

Mouth piece

Who is this woman and why is she so upbeat? Does she remind you of anyone you know? Set your timer for five and go!

What is he not saying? Who would be hurt if he said it? Who will be hurt if he doesn't say it? Set your timer for five and go!

Eye piece

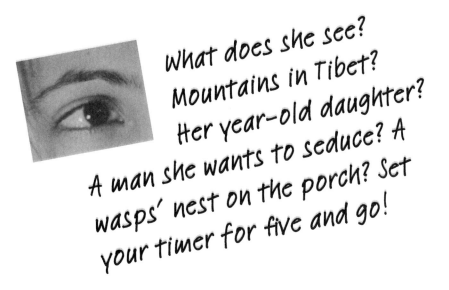

What sort of man is this? What does he want?
What stops him? What drives him? Does he remind
you of someone? Set your timer for five and go!

What does she see?
Mountains in Tibet?
Her year-old daughter?
A man she wants to seduce? A
wasps' nest on the porch? Set
your timer for five and go!

Found objects

What is unusual about these glasses? Set your timer for ten and write a piece. You might include where and how they were found, and by whom.

Combination piece

With closed eyes, point to an object on the left and a character on the right. Set your timer for fifteen and combine the two in a piece.

a leaky faucet	a war hero
a flat tire	a clairvoyant
a locked suitcase	an uptight lawyer
a cracked mirror	a CIA operative
one shoe	a tribal chief
a TV	a union organizer
a loose screw	a gardener
a raincoat	a feminist
a roll of film	a retarded boy
a shrunken head	a saleslady
a bracelet	a jokester
a dusty chain	a one-armed rebel

Hair piece

To whom does this strand of hair belong? Was it found in a sink? In someone's food? On a coat collar? Who found it? Is it proof of foul play? Set your timer for ten minutes and write a piece about the circumstances in which this hair was found.

What's in the box?

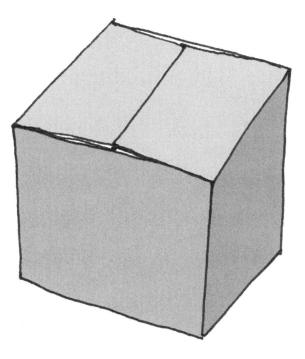

The box may be big enough to hold the Sahara Desert or small enough to hold a molecule of dust. Set your timer for five minutes and go.

Is she "real"?

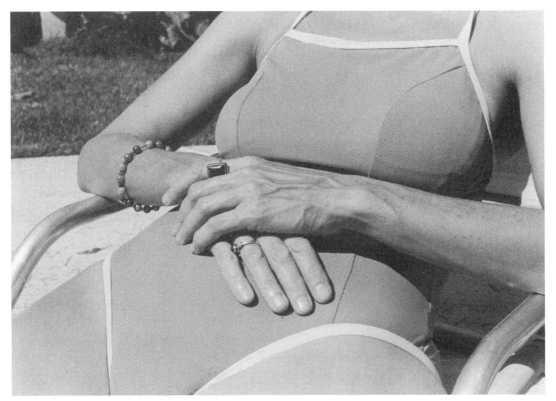

Who comes to mind when you look at the woman in this picture? Your father's third wife? The aunt of the little girl who drowned? Who else could she be? A grifter? A wealthy man's mistress? Quickly list on the left whoever comes to mind—whether that person is "real" or imagined. Choose the one with the most ENERGY, set your timer for twenty, and write a piece. Then choose one that is neutral, set your timer again for twenty, and go!

1. _____

2. _____

3. _____

4. _____

5. _____

6. _____

7. _____

8. _____

9. _____

10. _____

How are they connected?

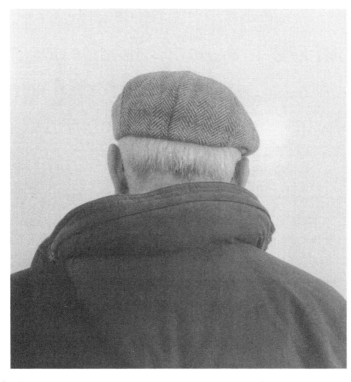

Do they both have secret loves? Are they Russian spies? Members of a secret sect? Heavy drinkers? Biologists? Postal workers? Were they both in a train accident?

Did they both experience a recent loss? Did they both receive large awards? Do they both have back problems? Set your timer for five and go.

Four silhouettes

These silhouettes do not look like the faces I drew when I was a child, though I was partial to profiles, especially to profiles of women. Women were easier for me to draw than men.

Do any of these silhouettes remind you of someone you know? If so, set your timer for five and write about that person.

If not, imagine these four people. Are they related? Do they all love the color turquoise? Do they suffer from asthma? What do they have in common? In what ways are they different? Set your timer for twenty and go.

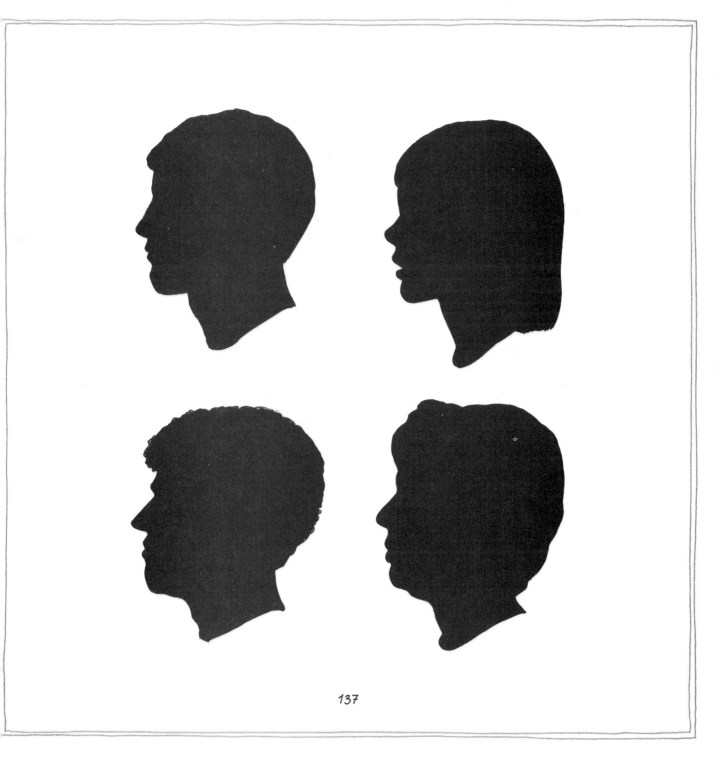

Who is she?

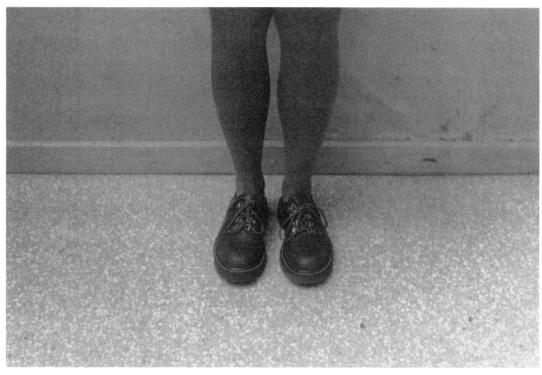

Does she remind you of anyone in your past? Anyone you know now? Set your timer for five minutes and write a piece about anyone who comes to mind when you look at this picture.

One of three women

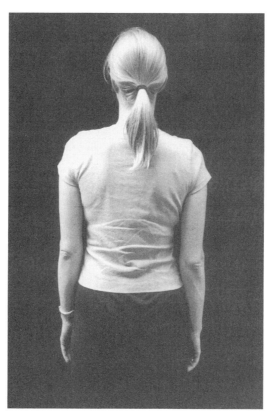

Where are the other two? Who are the other two? Who is this one? Set your timer for ten and write a piece about all three.

Pick a name

Choose the one from each column with the most ENERGY. Or if you don't feel drawn to any particular names, choose three at random by pointing to one in each column with closed eyes. Set your timer for ten minutes and write about all three.

Or you may choose the name of a person you know in each column. Write a ten-minute piece about all three. Or write a ten-minute piece about two of them. Or write about the one with the most ENERGY in an eight-minute piece.

1.

Diane
Robin
Richard
Margaret
William
Robert
Michael
Charles
Virginia
Ralph
Peter
Jeanie

2.

Tim
Hank
Susan
Fred
Marianne
Georgette
Carol
Thomas
Carolyn
Anne
Lorraine
Joe

3.

Sandra
Wallace
James
Lex
Sharon
Nancy
Donna
Linda
Sheila
John
Peggy
Ronald

Before . . .

Choose a number from 1 to 6. Set your timer for ten minutes. Write a piece beginning with the "before" phrase corresponding to your number.

1. Before the Texan could say another word . . .

2. Before the Chinese seamstress opened the letter . . .

3. Before the bowling team met for the last time . . .

4. Before the violinist and his wife left to have dinner . . .

5. Before she found the sapphire ring . . .

6. Before Annie sold the pet parlor . . .

After . . .

Choose a number from 1 to 6. Set your timer for ten minutes. Write a piece beginning with the "after" phrase corresponding to your number.

1. After he canceled the wedding . . .

2. After the dalmatian was lost . . .

3. After the Siamese twins were born . . .

4. After the Mercedes drove away . . .

5. After the old couple searched the house . . .

6. After Eric declined the lady wrestler's invitation . . .

Use this page to create your own "before" and "after" phrases. Do them fast! Then pick the one with the most ENERGY in either category and write a ten-minute piece.

Before _____

Before _____

Before _____

Before _____

After _____

After _____

After _____

After _____

Who is he?

What do his shoes tell you? His pants? The way
he is standing? Can you tell if he is intelligent?
Grateful? Annoyed? Set your timer for five
and go.

Where and who?

Write a piece connecting this place and this man.

Set your timer for ten minutes and go!

Pick a place

Quickly look through the lists. Choose the place with the most ENERGY. Or choose the place with the least ENERGY. Or choose a place with your eyes closed. Set your timer for five minutes and go.

Quickly look through the lists. Choose the group of four with the most ENERGY. Or choose the group of four with the least ENERGY. Or choose a group with your eyes closed. Set your timer for thirty minutes and write a piece connecting all four places.

a vacant lot in Queens
a cruise ship on its way to China
a city street
a beach littered with garbage

a field of wildflowers in Switzerland
a dark alley
an outdoor market
a public schoolyard

an escalator in a department store
a bar
a bait shop
a post office

a national park
the pyramids in Egypt
a university classroom
a crack house

a deserted railway station
a baseball field
a room in a transient hotel
an old mansion

a base camp in the Himalayas
a casino
a war-torn country
a locker room

a nuclear plant
a hospital
an airport waiting room
a liquor store in a poor neighborhood

an attic or cellar
a burning building
a zoo
a police station

More places

Quickly list the first eight that spring to mind.

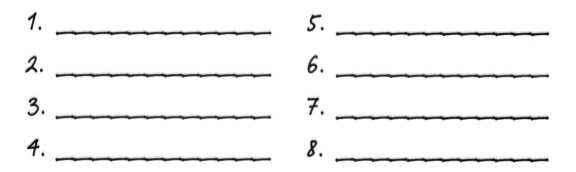

1. _____   5. _____

2. _____   6. _____

3. _____   7. _____

4. _____   8. _____

Choose the place with the most ENERGY, set your timer for ten, and write a piece.

You may also inject new life in an existing piece by changing the setting to one above. Or take an incident from a previous exercise and use it in one of these settings. Set your timer for ten and go.

A real place

Imagine yourself or a character you created in this landscape. What are you or your character doing? Why are you or your character here? Set your timer for fifteen and go.

Another real place

Imagine yourself or a character here. Who is with you or your character? What plans have been made? What problems exist? Set your timer for ten and go.

Islands

Imagine the shapes on the right as islands. Set your timer for fifteen minutes and write about one of them.

Describe the people.
Describe the plants and animals.
Describe the towns and cities and villages.
Describe the customs, the rituals.
Describe the wars.
Describe the mountains and rivers.
Describe the deserts, the lakes.
Describe the food, the chain hotels.
Describe the mines, the mineral deposits, the oil.
Describe the fog, the dampness, the rains, the
    heat, the sun.
Describe the earthquakes, volcanoes, floods.

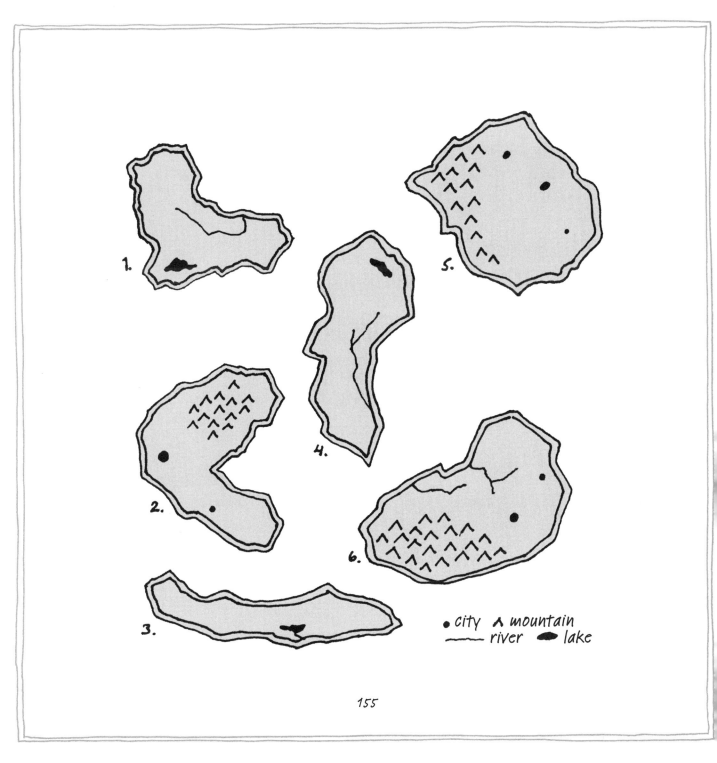

1.

2.

3.

4.

5.

6.

• city ∧ mountain
—— river 🐟 lake

155

What was lost here?

Set your timer for ten and go.

A primeval place

Imagine yourself, someone you know, or a character in this primeval place. What feelings come to mind? What thoughts? What incidents? Set your timer for fifteen and go.

Dream space

Imagine yourself floating in this dream space. Go wherever your mind takes you. Set your timer for twenty minutes and see where you end up.

Twenty-four figures

Look at the figures on the next two pages, then turn the page.

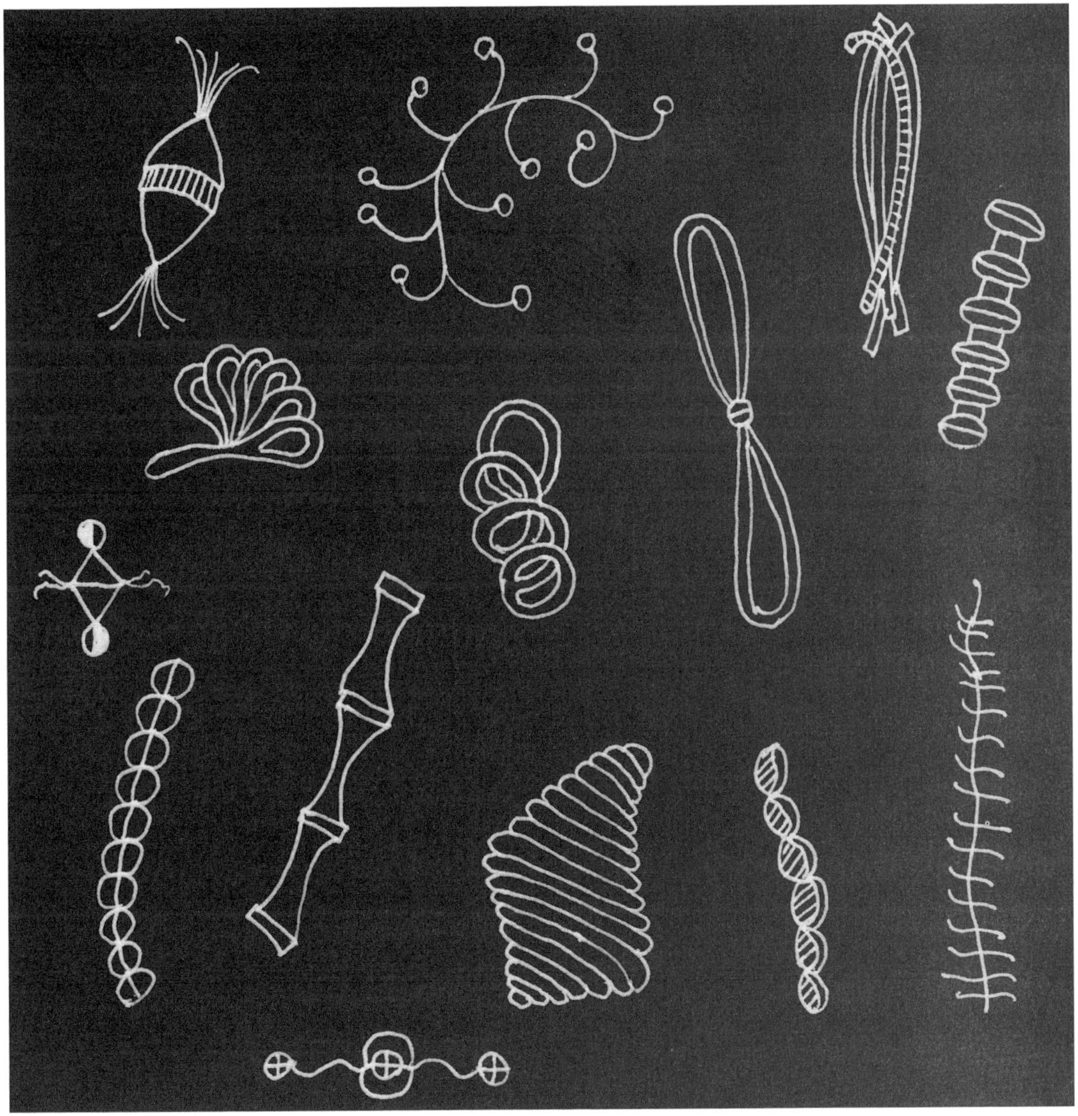

Write the first ten words that come to mind.

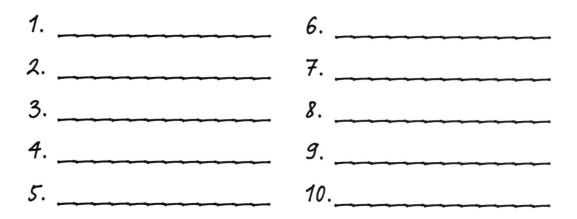

1. _____ 6. _____

2. _____ 7. _____

3. _____ 8. _____

4. _____ 9. _____

5. _____ 10._____

Set your timer for ten minutes and combine the two words with the most ENERGY in a piece.

Set your timer for five minutes and combine two neutral words in a piece.

More inspirations

Both the thesaurus and the dictionary can be inspiring when used on their own. Just turn to any page and choose a word with ENERGY or one at random as a topic for a five- or ten-minute exercise.

I once wrote a number of stories using a food dictionary to trigger ideas while designing a catalog for a French food firm.

Pick two numbers

Without looking at the following page, pick two numbers from 1 to 20. Then find the words that correspond to your chosen numbers and combine them in a piece. Set your timer for five minutes and go.

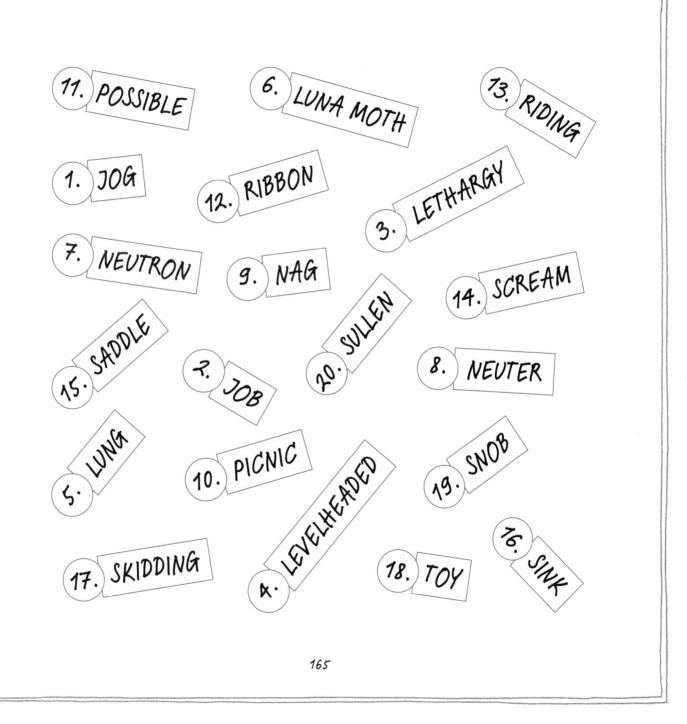

11. POSSIBLE

6. LUNA MOTH

13. RIDING

1. JOG

12. RIBBON

3. LETHARGY

7. NEUTRON

9. NAG

14. SCREAM

15. SADDLE

20. SULLEN

8. NEUTER

2. JOB

5. LUNG

10. PICNIC

19. SNOB

16. SINK

17. SKIDDING

4. LEVELHEADED

18. TOY

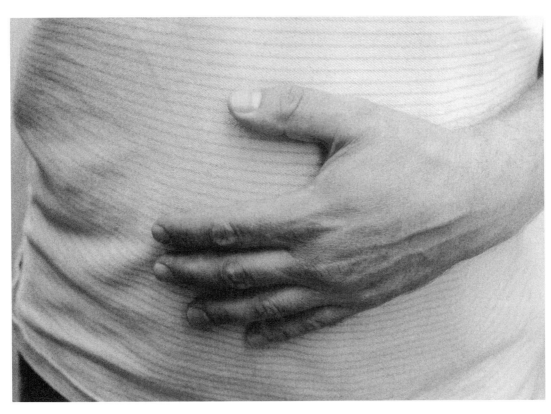

Whose hand is this? What has he touched?

Has he touched something . . .

soft?

papery?

spiny?

hard?

firm?

leathery?

slimy?

flabby?

cool?

silky?

gooey?

pointed?

velvety?

spongy?

round?

rough?

rubbery?

sticky?

smooth?

stringy?

viscous?

cold?

warm?

gummy?

hot?

prickly?

fuzzy?

icy?

damp?

Jell-O-like?

thin?

sharp?

grainy?

thick?

hairy?

Set your timer for twenty minutes and write a piece about the experience of touch.

What do they smell?

Grass?
Burnt rubber?
Varnish?
Aftershave?
Wood smoke?
Garbage?
Ammonia?
Pine?
Sweat?
Horse manure?
Eau de cologne?
Gas?
Incense?
Jasmine?
Roasted chestnuts?

Exhaust fumes?
Lilacs?
Camphor?
Eucalyptus?
Cigarettes?
Something else?

Who are "they"? Set your timer for ten and go!

Remember a good smell or a bad one. What were the circumstances? Set your timer for ten and go!

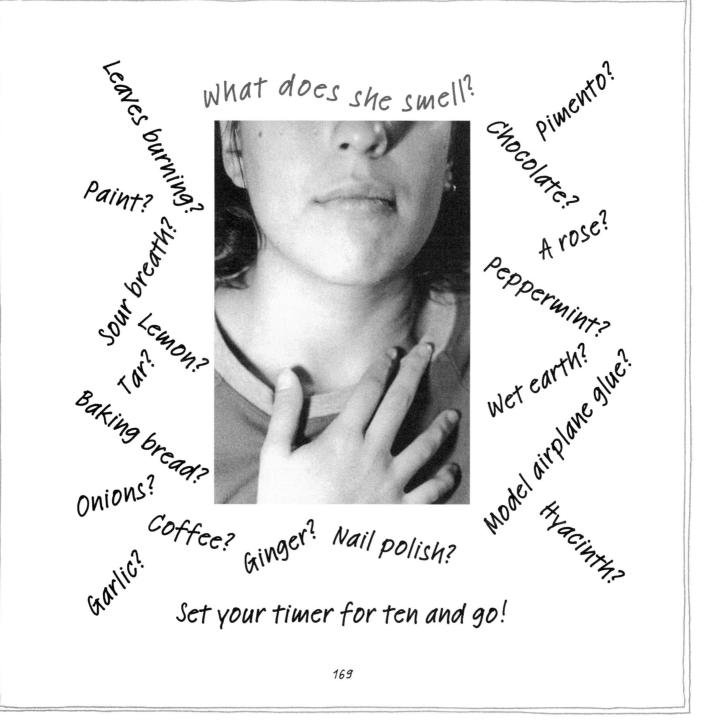

What does she smell?

Leaves burning?
Paint?
Sour breath?
Lemon?
Tar?
Baking bread?
Onions?
Garlic?
Coffee?
Ginger?
Nail polish?

Pimento?
Chocolate?
A rose?
Peppermint?
Wet earth?
Model airplane glue?
Hyacinth?

Set your timer for ten and go!

A bad taste?

What did she eat? Was it something rancid? Hot? Bitter? Spoiled? Spicy? Sharp? Sour? What were the circumstances? Set your timer for ten and write a piece.

Remember or imagine tasting something you love or hate. Set your timer again for ten and go.

Remember or imagine tasting something salty, tangy, pungent, tart, cold, burning, bland, savory, chalky, sugary, gamy, rich, unripe, stale, dry, nutty, curdled, or vinegary. Set your timer for ten and go.

Eavesdropping

Listen to people talking on the street, on the bus, at the bank, on their cell phones, in the subway, at work, at school, in the supermarket, at the movies, at the dry cleaners, in public bathrooms, in elevators, in hallways—wherever you go. Don't forget playgrounds or bars.

Jot down one line you hear each day for a week. Enter that line on the page at the right.

After the week is over, pick out the line with the most ENERGY and continue the conversation— any way you want—in a five- or ten- or twenty- minute piece.

day 1: _____

_____

day 2: _____

_____

day 3: _____

_____

day 4: _____

_____

day 5: _____

_____

day 6: _____

_____

day 7: _____

_____

Sound piece

Some writers are more inspired by what they hear than what they see. Are you one of them?

Choose the sound with the most ENERGY or choose one that leaves you cold. Keep in mind that a murmur may have more ENERGY for you than a shriek. Set your timer for ten and go!

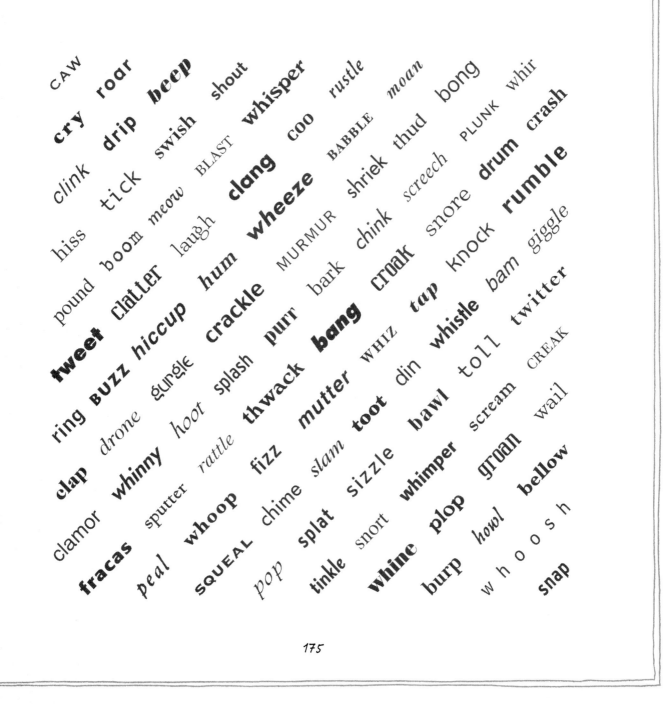

Pick an action

Set your timer for ten. Choose the action with the most ENERGY and write a piece.

Set your timer again for ten. Choose an action with your eyes closed or choose the one with the least ENERGY. And go!

kayak

light a match

fix a flat tire

draw

wash a car

double park

throw out the garbage

swim laps

swat flies

shovel snow

feed the cat

hum a tune

clean a closet

take a walk

take a pill

give birth

mow a lawn

take a trip

fry eggs

call a friend

kill a spider

change diapers

fly a plane

lift weights

eat a snack

have a drink

ride a bus

ride a bicycle

walk the dog

write a bad check

paint a room

steal a wallet

tell a story

cross a street

play poker

hide money

plant tomatoes

catch a mouse

sleepwalk

play blackjack

Pick an issue

Set your timer for ten minutes. Choose an issue that has little or no ENERGY (if there is one). Or write about one you don't know about. Write a piece from the viewpoint of a fictional character or from the viewpoint of someone you don't know well.

Set your timer for another ten minutes. Choose the issue with the most ENERGY and make it personal. If your pet issue isn't listed, use it instead of the ones presented here.

world hunger

gun control

racism

toxic dumps

abortion rights

free speech

women's rights

global warming

illiteracy

saving the environment

terrorism

capital punishment

land mines

nuclear testing

biochemical warfare

drug abuse

aging

gay rights

Pick an animal

I remember the first time I saw a platypus at the Bronx Zoo. I was a child in awe, staring at a furry little creature with webbed feet and a ducklike bill swimming in a pool.

Do you remember the first time you saw a gorilla? A lion? A snake under the porch or in the woods?

Set your timer for five and write a piece about the animal with the most ENERGY, or write a piece about an animal you've never seen or know little about.

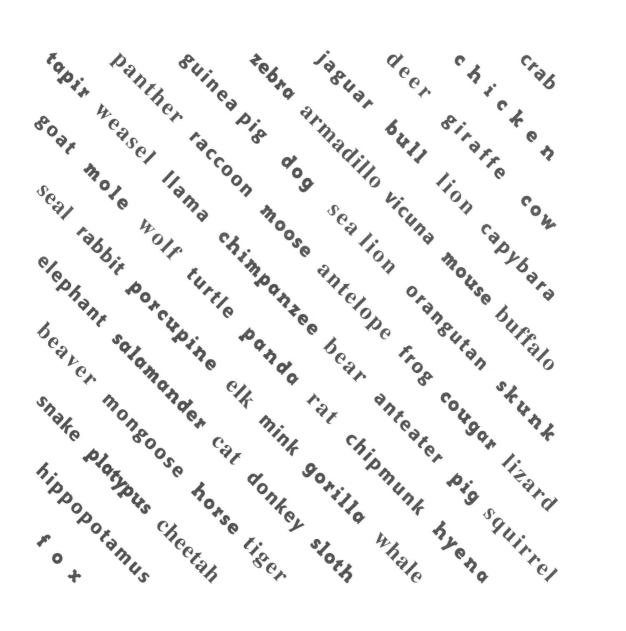

Pick a noun

Pick the one with the most or least ENERGY. Or pick one with your eyes closed. Set your timer for five and write a piece about it.

Pick three with your eyes closed and combine them in a ten-minute piece.

Pick one that stays in your mind when you look away and write about it for ten minutes.

More lines

I drew these lines very fast, then slowly filled in some of the shapes made by the intersecting lines. What do you see when you look at this drawing? Set your timer for five and go.

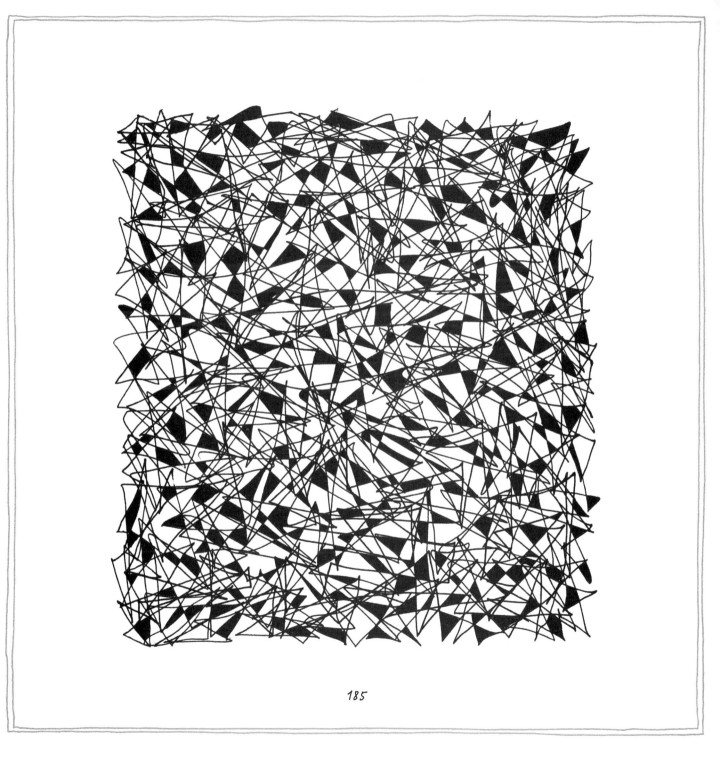

185

Drawing lines

On the next page, take a pen or pencil and draw a picture with lines. They may be thick or thin, straight or wavy, long or short. You may draw them fast or slowly. You may draw just a few or many. You may connect them or not.

When you're finished, write the first three sentences that come to mind.

1. _____

2. _____

3. _____

Use the sentence with the most ENERGY as the subject of a piece. Set your timer for ten and go.

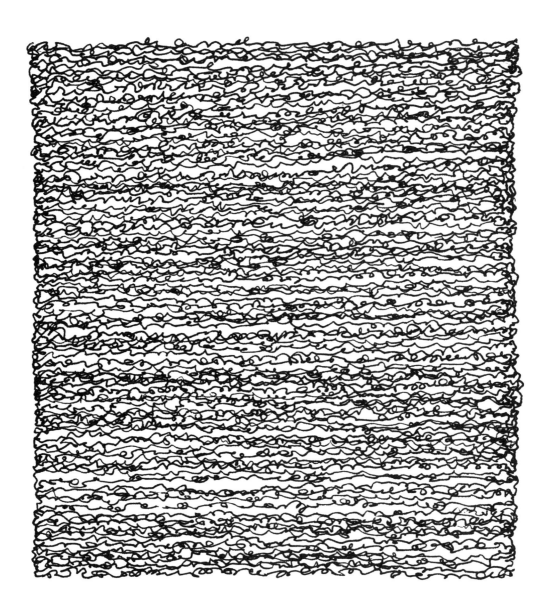

188

Cryptic writing

Imagine this as a form of cryptic writing you are able to decode. What tale is being told? Set your timer for twenty minutes and tell it in your own words.

Now what?

So you've gone through the entire book? Now what? you ask. You can, of course, go back over the exercises. Each time you'll get different results. You can use the book over and over.

But you can do other things too. Just remember, as you read the following pages, to set your timer whenever you do an exercise. Remember, the timer creates pressure, draws ENERGY to the surface.

Collect pictures (without captions) that have ENERGY for you. You may be attracted by the color or subject matter or style of the photographs and illustrations you choose. Find them in magazines, newspapers, catalogs, or on postcards. Keep them in a special file or scrapbook.

Collect objects that have ENERGY for you: that fit in your hand and appeal to your sense of sight or touch or both. A bead, a swatch of cloth, seashells, stones, bits of colored glass, mementos from trips — these are some examples. Keep them in a box.

<u>Collect headlines and small articles</u> that have ENERGY for you. Find them in magazines, newspapers. Keep them in a file or scrapbook.

<u>Collect snapshots</u> that have ENERGY for you. They may be from trips. Or they may be pictures of family or friends. They can be old photos of generations long gone or snapshots of strangers found at a flea market. Keep them in a file, or scrapbook, or box.

<u>Collect spoken material</u> that has ENERGY for you. Keep a notebook of things said to you, things you overhear. On TV and radio—talk shows, sitcoms, crime dramas—you may find lines that move you. Jot them down.

Collect words and phrases that have ENERGY for you. Thumb through dictionaries and different kinds of encyclopedias. Old animal encyclopedias inspire me. Keep your words and phrases in a notebook.

Collect moments that have ENERGY for you. Start by changing your routine. Take a new route to work or school. Wake up earlier. Listen to a different radio program. Watch a different channel on TV. Read a book or magazine you normally wouldn't read. Do something unusual. Go bowling. Or play miniature golf. Or go to the opera. Or take a walk in an unfamiliar neighborhood.

What's the point? To wake yourself up to the HERE and NOW: to the PRESENT MOMENT. Notice your surroundings. Notice how you feel. Keep a notebook and jot down those moments of ENERGY.

This morning, for example, when I walked over to my open window and breathed in the summer air, it smelled unusually sweet. A fresh breeze blew. I felt suddenly alive: deeply aware that all was right in my life. These moments happen — if you let them — even at times when the world may be in turmoil. These are the moments when you are in touch with that ENERGY, which is life itself.

How to run a Playful Way group

When two or more people come together to do Playful Way exercises, they generate ENERGY. In a group of six to eight, there is even more ENERGY. Imagine what a group of one hundred would be like! GROUP ENERGY is VERY POWERFUL!

What you need to form a group are people familiar with the ENERGY METHOD who are willing to share and support one another.

As a group, you need to decide when, where, how often you will meet, and how long a meeting should be. You need to choose a leader to call people and set it up. You may rotate the leadership from session to session.

Each member should bring to each meeting a copy of *The Playful Way to Serious Writing*. If the group isn't too big, each member should have the opportunity to select an exercise for the group at each session. DON'T CHOOSE EXERCISES IN ADVANCE!

In a group larger than four, I suggest keeping the exercises down to ten minutes or less to make sure that everyone who wants to read aloud gets a chance.

You may try sharing personal pieces (on fears and memories, for instance) in pairs instead of sharing them with everyone. When sharing, it may be helpful to tell the reader which parts were most interesting, which parts – in your opinion – might be developed more.

By this time, I think you know that every exercise holds the ENERGY you bring to it. So have fun and let the ENERGY flow!

If you would like me to run a Playful Way workshop or seminar, please e-mail me at Robertaallen7@aol.com. You may also visit my Web site: http://hometown.aol.com/Roall.

Acknowledgments

I wish to thank Lorrie Bodger for her generosity, enthusiasm, and excellent advice. Joel Agee, whom I've never before thanked in print, once again offered valuable suggestions. I wish to thank my editor, Susan Canavan, for giving me the freedom to take this project as far as I could go. I would also like to acknowledge my supportive agent, DeAnna Heindel. And last but not least, Craig.

JERRY BAUER

Roberta Allen is the author of two collections of stories, <u>The Traveling Woman</u> and <u>Certain People</u>; a novella in stories, <u>The Daughter</u>; a novel, <u>The Dreaming Girl</u>; a travel memoir, <u>Amazon Dream</u>; and a writing guide, <u>Fast Fiction: Creating Fiction in Five Minutes</u>. Allen is on the faculty of the New School University and has taught in the writing program at Columbia University and in numerous private workshops. She is also a visual artist who has exhibited worldwide, with work in the collection of the Metropolitan Museum of Art and Bibliotheque du France, Paris. She lives in New York City.